## About Demos

Demos is a greenhouse for new ideas which can improve the quality of our lives. As an independent think tank, we aim to create an open resource of knowledge and learning that operates beyond traditional party politics.

We connect researchers, thinkers and practitioners to an international network of people changing politics. Our ideas regularly influence government policy, but we also work with companies, NGOs, colleges and professional bodies.

Demos knowledge is organised around five themes, which combine to create new perspectives. The themes are democracy, learning, enterprise, quality of life and global change.

But we also understand that thinking by itself is not enough. Demos has helped to initiate a number of practical projects which are delivering real social benefit through the redesign of public services.

We bring together people from a wide range of backgrounds to cross-fertilise ideas and experience. By working with Demos, our partners develop a sharper insight into the way ideas shape society. For Demos, the process is as important as the final product.

**www.demos.co.uk**

First published in 2003
© Demos
All rights reserved

ISBN 1 84180 111 9
Typeset by Special Edition Pre-press Services, mail@special-edition.co.uk
Cover design by Politico's Design, design@politicos.co.uk
Printed by Printflow, London

For further information and
subscription details please contact:

Demos
The Mezzanine
Elizabeth House
39 York Road
London SE1 7NQ

telephone: 020 7401 5330
email: mail@demos.co.uk
web: www.demos.co.uk

# Education Epidemic

## Transforming secondary schools through innovation networks

David H Hargreaves

**DEMOS**

# Contents

**Transforming public services** · A Demos work programme

Demos is generating new ideas and practice which can help public service organisations adapt in changing society. In the process, we are developing a deeper understanding of how organisations learn, and how policy and practice interact in an interconnected world.

We work in partnership with many organisations, ranging from public agencies and government departments to trade unions, charities, community and practitioner organisations.

Our current partners include: Centrex; the Netherlands Ministry of Justice; the Department of Premier and Cabinet in Victoria, Australia; Creative Partnerships; Scottish Enterprise; NHS University; North Southwark Education Action Zone; DEFRA; DTI and DfES.

In education, Demos is working as a strategic partner to the National College for School Leadership (NCSL) and its networked learning group. This project is implementing some of the ideas at the heart of David Hargreaves' pamphlet.

By bridging the artificial divides between policy and practice, Demos has placed itself at the forefront of a new approach to transforming public services. This approach recognises that policy-makers and politicians operate within the same system as practitioners and service users.

Our aim is not only to generate ideas and recommendations through research and publications (see below), but also to help create the strategies through which ideas and practice can merge. This approach can help reconcile the apparently competing demands for local autonomy and governments' desire to drive change from the centre.

Demos draws extensively on systems thinking. This is a mature discipline in science and technology but is only now being applied to public policy-making. In the year since it was published, System Failure has created a significant impact in policy-making circles and has led to a new Demos research programme, including a major project on regulation.

Public service reform and democratic renewal are generally understood as different problems requiring different solutions. By thinking about what public service users want, and the effort they are prepared to commit to getting it, Demos is also describing a new form of political engagement, which is expressed locally but has national implications.

This bottom-up form of organisation – known as emergence – is understood in natural systems, but is being developed by Demos as an approach to democratic renewal through self-government.

**Open Source Democracy** • Douglas Rushkoff, 2003 (forthcoming)
*The peer-to-peer communication online has created new forms of interactions, which could create a new form of networked democracy.*

**People Flow** • Theo Veenkamp, Alessandra Buonfino, Tom Bentley, 2003
*Only by understanding the drivers for international people movement can a management system be developed to absorb the pressure they create.*

**Innovate from Within** • Charles Leadbeater, 2002
*Civil service reform is a prerequisite for transforming public services.*

**System Failure** • Jake Chapman, 2002
*The law of unintended consequences will always prevail in any attempt to change organisations by command or clever public policy instrument.*

**Gaia: the new big idea** • Mary Midgley, 2001
*Nature has as much to teach us about cooperation as it does about competition in whole systems, from economies to eco-systems.*

**Classroom Assistance** • Matthew Horne, 2001
*The progressive transformation of the education system means harnessing the professional capabilities of teachers, and tackling recruitment problems in the process.*

**It's Democracy, Stupid** • Tom Bentley, 2001
*Political disengagement should NOT be mistaken for voter apathy; the public can be reengaged by giving them a more direct role in democracy, or self-governance.*

**Creative Professionalism** • David Hargreaves, 1998
*Understanding how we learn to learn is a necessary condition for developing effective teaching for a knowledge economy.*

**Holistic Government** • Perri 6, 1997
*The pamphlet that developed the concept of 'joined-up government' also set out the basis for thinking about how governments can become learning organisations.*

**The Society of Networks** • Geoff Mulgan and Ivan Briscoe, 1995
*The information age implies a need for new kinds of network-based organisations, which can rapidly adapt to social, economic and technological changes.*

**The Mosaic of Learning** • David Hargreaves, 1994
*The comprehensive school may be in decline, but not the comprehensive principle; more diversity and parental choice will be a positive force in education.*

# Acknowledgements

I am deeply grateful to Owen Lynch and to Tom Bentley and Demos staff for their insightful suggestions and cogent criticisms of an earlier draft.

# Foreword

Six years into the UK's New Labour government, public services are approaching another crossroads. Government-by-target is widely accepted to have reached its limits as a strategy. Targets are still an essential part of the toolkit, but setting linear improvement goals and then pushing hard to achieve them can no longer be the dominant principle for reforming large, partly autonomous organisations. But the pragmatic delivery focus of earlier years is being replaced by even more ambitious objectives, along with more intense disputes over the costs and consequences of reform.

As a result, a government that began by insisting that 'standards, not structures' mattered most is now staking its credibility on the introduction of new structures, including foundation hospitals and specialist schools.

Politically, public services are the focus of a wider struggle to prove that amid growing diversity and inequality, public investment and intervention are part of what holds society together. The contention is that a strong public realm can equip us all to thrive in a rapidly changing society, and help make social fairness and cohesion a reality. The stakes could hardly be higher.

That is why the growing use of 'transformation' as a goal is so important. Recent reform has shown that short-term improvements in key areas such as numeracy and literacy scores, hospital waiting times and street crime are possible. But embedding higher expectations and performance permanently in the workings of public service organisations means changing 'whole systems', often radically, and equipping them to adapt more effectively to ongoing change.

This is the essential challenge facing every government which seeks actively to influence the society that elected it. Is it possible to conceive, deliver and legitimate large-scale programmes of change, reflecting collective goals, in societies where ideological prescription is weak and fuzzy and institutions seem beset by diversity, complexity and fragmentation? Public appetite for better services has not diminished. But the changing social landscape means that public or *shared* solutions must be increasingly personalised to suit individual needs and expectations.

For reformers concerned with both excellence *and* equity, the question can be put more simply: how can government strategy combine diverse provision with holism, or the ability to generate some universal standards of expectation and outcome? How can the provision of public services uniquely for each person be reconciled with the ongoing need to cater for *all* people?

The tendency for reformers – in all sectors – is to rely on formal restructuring of organisational relationships: new structures, new powers and new rules to encourage higher performance. But when the most important information is often distributed very widely across sectors, communities and the wider social environment, formal structures are a limited part of the picture. In fact we need complex systems of organisation and provision to be capable of adapting *as systems* to new demands and new possibilities. And if they are to be embedded permanently in communities, and be genuinely responsive to them, they must be able to sustain this process of adaptation on their own.

To achieve coherence and democratic legitimacy, real 'transformation' must be politically led and shaped by public values. But it must also affect people and cultures far beyond those organisations nominally controlled by government. This is probably the biggest challenge to our mental models of 'reform'. Somehow, reform of public service organisations needs to dedicate them to social outcomes beyond the reach of their formal accountability. There is no other way to achieve the full potential, or entitlement, of all citizens in complex and diverse societies.

In recent history, public service reform has used twentieth-century organisational techniques to improve the productivity of nineteenth-century institutions. In education performance management, targeting, change management, local competition and professional development tools have all been used to improve the 'output' of schooling. But while the language and tools have changed considerably, the basic institutional parameters of schools have changed relatively little. The same could be said for GPs, hospitals, police forces, social services or most other core public services.

The underlying concept of performance is not unique to this government. As David Hargreaves argues, it rests on the 'input–process–output' model inherited from the twentieth century's extraordinarily powerful definitions of how modern organisations work.

In all the major services, the 'resilience' of the core institutions is usually taken for granted. It is sustained by public expectations, funding legacies, professional culture and standing structures of accountability and control. The people who work in them participate in processes of continuous adaptation in order to preserve the systems and sustain their own roles. That means incorporating new language, technology, knowledge and expectations, and responding incrementally to change in their external environment.

But meeting public need in the twenty-first century requires different organisations with different functions to work together systematically, for example across boundaries between health, housing and learning. It also requires resilient institutions to interact far more creatively with the resources – social, economic, cultural and knowledge-based – that surround them in local communities. It is the combination of individual behaviour, social context and formal organisational process that produces a radically improved outcome. This kind of innovation will not change whole services without its results being spread rapidly across large systems.

This is a tall order. But there is no reason to think it is impossible. What is impossible, however, is that such a complex and open-ended process could be successfully directed or controlled by any one privileged source of knowledge, energy or power.

In reality, hardly anybody believes solely in a 'command and control' model of coordination. In its pure form, it is a myth. But nonetheless a large amount of the structure and culture of government rests on a model of control and accountability designed to reflect that fiction.

Much of what is happening in education, health, social security and criminal justice represents an attempt to make the systems work more intelligently, while also improving basic performance and efficiency. But in the process, often invisibly to those involved, the effort itself is impeded by the limitations of organisational design.

Thus the coming idea of *intelligent accountability* cannot be effectively implemented if producers are held to account only within existing institutional structures. 'Intelligence' has to mean responsiveness to local circumstances and the capacity to be demanding and rigorous while accommodating the risks of innovation. This capacity can only be generated by bringing together many different perspectives in intelligent ways.

In this pamphlet, David Hargreaves argues that transformation could occur by shaping and stimulating *disciplined* processes of innovation within the school system, and building an infrastructure capable of transferring ideas, knowledge and new practices *laterally* across it.

Huge amounts of money, time and effort are spent trying to spread 'good' and 'recommended' practice more widely across embedded systems of organisation. Most of that effort is wasted, because what we already know about how such transfer occurs (which is not enough) is not used in the design of dissemination strategies.

The organisational form that can give depth and scale to this kind of exchange is the network. Hargreaves shows how, with the right kind of leadership and governance, the formation of networks combining collaborative and competitive endeavour could play a vital role in creating world class, adaptive public services.

Knowledge-based networks are not the alternative to existing forms of public provision: they are an essential complement. Rather than being represented by an organisational structure or a single policy lever, transformation becomes an 'emergent property' of the whole system as it learns to generate, incorporate and adapt to the best of the specific new ideas and practices that get thrown up around it.

Complexity and unintended outcomes are already features of our public services, as recent crises over exam marking and school funding have vividly shown. The challenge is not to eliminate them, but to build a system capable of thriving on the diverse and complex sources of knowledge and information with which it has to contend.

In education, despite recent turbulence, reform has put in place a set of foundations for what could become genuinely radical change. They include the early improvements in the basics, the creation of an ICT infrastructure, a national foundation for early years, reshaping of the teaching profession and plans to remodel 14–19 provision.

One familiar response to the difficulty of directing change has always been that government should 'trust the professionals'. Many public service professionals still feel that if they could just be left to get on with the job, they would be able to perform successfully. Unfortunately, this is not the case either. Professionals, just like organisations, are as likely to resort to self-protection in the face of disruptive change as they are to embrace new and better practices. The challenge is to build professional identities and learning communities that are oriented towards adaptation and radical innovation. Again, these identities will emerge in part through networks.

The education narrative is already moving from an emphasis on 'informed prescription' towards 'informed professionalism' as the basis for improvement. But by what, or whom, should professionals be informed and challenged to adapt? The depth of the challenge means that they should be radically challenged by it. Its complexity means that they should be informed and supported by a system capable of rapidly transferring many different kinds of knowledge.

As Hargreaves concludes, the big challenge is for systems like education to work out how to learn for themselves. And if their goal is equity as well as excellence, they must learn how to meet the needs of people they have never successfully served, as well as to operate at the leading edge of pedagogical and organisational innovation. In fact, one may imply the other.

The central idea should not be to select one form of organisation and impose or replicate it. It should be to create systems that challenge and motivate a critical mass of participants, and provide the capacity to reinvent the structures and practices from within.

With this in mind, the contours of a transformed education system are coming into view. Its major features will include:

O   many dynamic networks of schools and other providers operating collaboratively across local areas, perhaps in competition with each other

O   a new 'network infrastructure' of local and regional intermediary organisations, often incorporating Local Education Authorities and Local Learning and Skills Councils, dedicated to improving system capacity and accountable for improving the quality and pace of system learning

O   rich, extended models of school organisation using networks and highly varied forms of learning to engage directly with wider communities and jointly produce the wider conditions under which successful educational attainment and learning take place

O   a reshaped Early Years sector, understood as the bedrock of all other educational and lifelong learning achievement, treated as a priority investment and acting as part of a seamless system of community support and social capital building

O   a teaching force encompassing a far wider range of expertise, with radically improved skills in innovation, data handling and use of research knowledge, and the ability to adopt and adapt teaching strategies designed for diverse learners and purposes

O   leadership capacity distributed widely across high performing schools and community networks, generating

consent for radical innovation and sustaining high
expectations

O ICT capacity used to provide personalised, real-time
information about student progress, as well as to offer
content and feedback in more flexible ways

O a reshaped system of central governance with clear and
simple objectives, underpinning a different kind of system-
wide capacity: to handle and shape the flow of knowledge,
information and capacity around the system, and make a
priority of the most intractable or urgent challenges, even
where they may disrupt.

Life in this new system may not be any calmer than at present, but it
could become more coherent. One implication of constant adaptation
may be that 'permanent revolution' should be accepted as the norm in
organisational life. The payoff is that a series of initiatives that bend the
performance of resilient systems could be replaced with a continuous
effort to equip the system to learn for itself.

To succeed, this kind of strategy will have to answer many difficult
questions as it develops, and make the answers widely available.
Questions include:

O How are networks generated and sustained?

O What forms of organisation are best suited to spreading
knowledge and energy widely across large-scale systems?

O What are the educational priorities with greatest potential
to focus people's efforts to innovate, and to create leverage
and legitimacy for wider change?

O What strategies for cultural change can policy-makers
legitimately add to their repertoire of tools for intervention?

O What roles can service users adopt to aid the innovation
and adaptation of service organisations?

O How can local governance systems learn to operate more
dynamically and effectively through lateral collaboration?

O What are the processes for evaluating and disciplining
innovation across distributed systems?

These are questions that Demos is seeking to answer through its own network of partnerships with governments, schools, public agencies, voluntary and community organisations. We hope they will contribute to a new politics of innovation and an agenda for transformation, which could yet have a profound and lasting effect on the future role and value of our public services.

Tom Bentley
Director, Demos
June 2003

# 1. Introduction

In 1983 I was invited by the Inner London Education Authority (ILEA) to chair an enquiry into under-performance in London's secondary schools. After extensive discussion with heads, teachers and other stakeholders, our committee published its report, *Improving Secondary Schools*, which somewhat to our surprise was read far beyond the ILEA. In retrospect, the report was a landmark in the development of a national agenda for improving schools. There were three reasons for this: it helped to define the issues on which the school improvement agenda would be based; it provided a focus for the growing conviction that the quality of secondary schooling could, and should, be improved; and it concentrated the analysis, rationale and evidence into a form (the report) that was widely accessible and could be transferred to other settings.

Twenty years later, the government is looking afresh at the reform of secondary schools, and we appear to be entering another, relatively rare, period of transition in which the basic parameters of the agenda for reform are once again changing. At the forefront, from the government's perspective, are the Key Stage 3 strategy, covering the 11–14 age range, and the plan for a coherent 14–19 phase, through a series of reforms over the next decade. For secondary schools, two recent documents, *A New Specialist System: Transforming secondary education*[1] and *The London Challenge: Transforming London secondary schools*[2] chart the way forward.

These are not just the latest stage in the long road to school improvement, but a significant change in direction. First, the language has changed: *improvement* has given way to *transformation*. What precisely does this mean? What accounts for the new language? Is the change justified? What difference will it make in practice? Secondly, there is a policy shift from 'standards not structures' to 'new structures for higher standards'. In 1997, David Blunkett published *Excellence in Schools*, which bluntly argued that:

> Standards matter more than structures. The preoccupation with school structure has absorbed a great deal of energy to little effect. We know what it takes to create a good school: a strong, skilled head who understands the importance of clear leadership, committed staff and parents, high expectations of every child and above all good teaching. These characteristics cannot be put in place by altering school structure or by legislation and financial pressure alone. Effective change in a field as dependent on human interaction as education requires millions of people to change their behaviour. That will require consistent advocacy and persuasion to create a climate in which schools are constantly challenged to compare themselves to other similar schools and adopt proven ways of raising their performance.[3]

By contrast, in his preface to *The London Challenge* Tony Blair immediately concedes that:

> Piecemeal change is not enough to build a first-class education system for London. Radical structural reform is essential, not only to raise standards in existing schools, but to reshape the system around diversity, choice and the new specialist principle ... Nowhere is the challenge to create this new system greater than in Inner London – and we need a level of innovation and reform to match.[4]

The confidence that the government had enough knowledge to raise standards and that this had nothing to do with structures, which were merely a debilitating distraction, has given way to a conviction that structural reform is now critical, that it has to be radical and be matched by innovation, presumably radical too. There is no explicit strategy for this ambitious programme of innovation; indeed, there is a lurking suspicion that advocating it too loudly might unleash a 1960s wave of anarchic innovation leading nowhere. At the same time this shift does not mark a return to an approach in which all consequential change in the system arises from the redesign of formal structures by central architects of policy or ideology. What seems to be emerging is a far more open-ended process, which combines action at many different levels of the system in coherent, purposeful ways. The most important characteristics of this process are not yet clear.

This pamphlet examines what might be meant by transformation and how it might be achieved. It is not a critique of government policy, old or new, in secondary education. It suggests, however, that the government's latest strategies are still insufficient to achieve the intended transformation. This, I believe, does indeed depend on 'human interaction as education requires millions of people to change their behaviour' and in turn this requires some different, if complementary, strategies. They will demand a different kind of leadership from the centre; new, disciplined responsibilities from school leaders; and new roles and organisation from the 'middle tier', currently occupied by the Local Education Authorities (LEAs) and Local Learning and Skills Councils (LLSCs). We must all acknowledge the limits of central interventions and capitalise rather on the power and commitment of the professionals and others with local knowledge to work the magic that makes a sustained and disciplined transformation.

Transformation is indeed needed in the next stage of educational reform. There are external and internal drivers of this need for deep change. The external driver is the recognition by many countries that as we enter a knowledge-based economy, more people should be better educated than ever before. States now compete more actively than ever to create 'world-class' education systems. Thus the recent international survey of OECD countries, known as PISA, has caused widespread interest as well as policy changes in many countries.[5] England did rather better than usual in this international league table, but being in the 'top ten' for the achievement of 15-year-olds in literacy, mathematics and science still leaves us significantly behind the leaders.

# 2. The challenge to strategy

The English government was pleased with these better than expected PISA results, in contrast with the dismay and alarm felt by Germany to their unexpected lower ranking. In Norway the education minister is following a top-down, centralist intervention not unlike that which has taken place in England over recent years and which has been interpreted as the cause of the improvement in student performance. At the same time, those at the top of such league tables, notably Japan and other East Asian countries, are far from complacent and are ready to innovate, not merely to maintain their position but to forge further ahead. All education systems now look on innovation more favourably; this explains why in England ministers have established an innovation unit in the Department for Education and Skills (DfES). In East Asia it is known that radical innovation in the way organisations work can transform an industry. They are now thinking hard about how educational organisations might engage in innovation to nurture the creativity on which their future success as a nation may well depend. The PISA-induced complacency has been short-lived in England, where ministers have become used, with some justification, to proclaiming internationally the success of reforms such as the literacy and numeracy strategies. The recent failure to maintain the upward curve of improvement has come as a shock. Is there something wrong with the strategies, ask ministers and their officials? Are some people, such as school principals or headteachers, or teacher trainers, not doing what they are supposed to do? Or is something more innovative required? Do we need a transformation rather than just improvement if we are to maintain our position in the PISA league table, let alone improve it?

As many countries across the world begin to invest in educational innovation, this is a time at which to apply Revans' Law to the education service: for an organisation to prosper, its rate of learning must be at least equal to the rate of change in the external environment. As the rate of change accelerates outside this country, schools and the DfES must improve their capacity to learn. If institutions at either local or national level fail to learn, we shall fall behind.

There are also internal drivers towards transformation. The first, which has already been taken seriously in South East Asian countries, is the recognition that in a knowledge economy more people need to be more creative and this will in itself require new approaches to teaching. In the words of a joint paper from the DTI and DfEE:

> People who generate bright ideas and have the practical abilities to turn them into successful products and services are vital not just to the creative industries but to every sector of business. Our whole approach to what and how we learn, from the earliest stages of learning, needs to adapt and change in response to this need. Academic achievement remains essential but it must increasingly be delivered through a rounded education which fosters creativity, enterprise and innovation ... [and this] depends on the very highest standards of teaching and learning and on the ability of teachers and lecturers to enhance the way young people learn so as to develop those capabilities ... We will foster creativity and enterprise across our education and training system through radical new approaches to teaching and learning.[6]

England sought to reach the levels of literacy and numeracy that had been achieved in Germany and some South East Asian countries. Without any reduction of the pressure on the basics, we must also now aspire to nurture through education the new qualities of creativity, innovation and enterprise, as more young people become knowledge workers of various kinds.

A second driver is the growing recognition that the improvement strategies hitherto adopted have inevitable limitations. Between 1997 and 2002, the literacy and numeracy strategies in primary schools were among the most impressive of the government's achievements in education. But the rate of improvement has levelled off. The literacy and numeracy strategies were a new top-down, highly prescriptive lever, which despite much early opposition to this undoubted challenge to the professional autonomy of primary school teachers has on the whole worked, though research is indicating that, while teachers like the strategy, the improved results are derived from teaching to the test rather than teaching better. All levers have their limits. Educational processes are complex, affected by many variables, so the amount of improvement any single lever can effect is smaller than reformers might wish. Moreover, when a new lever has a demonstrable positive impact, policy-makers tend to push the lever beyond its potential. For example, in England 'targets' – for students, teachers, schools, LEAs – have had a real effect on raising standards, but when targets work policy-makers impose yet more of them. The danger, of course, is that this can induce resistance to the very notion of a target and thus ruin what was originally an effective lever. Rather than pushing an old lever beyond its natural limits, policy-makers would be wise to search for new levers to replace older ones, not just additional ones. Charles Clarke's adoption of a more flexible view of targets and tests in primary schools had to be carefully presented to the public, as well as to teachers, as a change that did not mean he was going soft on standards: what one newspaper called a 'brave and far-sighted decision' was denounced in another as 'craven capitulation'. Appearing to abandon a lever is risky; explicitly replacing it by a better one makes professional good sense and a less vulnerable news item.

A third driver is that the improvements achieved thus far have not narrowed the gap in education achievement between the most and the least advantaged at the expected rate. We have known for over 20 years that whenever educational opportunities are increased, the middle classes take disproportionate advantage of them. For example, the huge expansion of higher education over this period has benefited middle class students more than working class students. A Labour government committed to closing the gap, rather than merely narrowing it, may well have to consider whether radical innovative measures are needed if this ambition is to be achieved. There are some real achievements by the government, for example in sharply reducing the number of 'failing' schools and those in special measures, and for Excellence in Cities. But the latest policy documents on secondary education, and especially secondary schools in London, make it clear that much more has to be done to close the gap.

A fourth driver is the difficulty of changing upper secondary education by means of a DfES centrally devised and imposed master-plan. Primary schools were a comparatively stable and coherent system, with teachers who are relatively responsive to central direction. By contrast, arrangements for the 14–19 age range involve many different types of institution, whose goals, ethos, histories and funding are very diverse. This is a complex, dynamic system in which it is much more difficult to engineer consent and change. Local variations in 14–19 needs, conditions, structures and cultures mean that the changes will be more idiosyncratic, and will need to be devised and implemented locally, with guidance and support from the centre, rather than constraint and control.

Transformation suggests that the improvement of secondary schools must be both deeper and faster than before. On this I agree with the government. But I am not convinced that it has all the right strategies in place to deliver the transformation. Can a more locally determined set of reforms for secondary schools be achieved with as much success, and in a similar timeframe of about five years, as the nationally determined strategies for the improvement of primary schools? And might such a strategy be used in several areas of reform, and as a complementary strategy in areas where the top-down, prescriptive strategies are reaching their natural limits? I offer a positive answer to these questions and suggest some key ingredients for the next stage of reform.

# 3. Mobilising capital – a new approach to school effectiveness

The last 25 years of school improvement strategies and policies has been based on an input–process–output model of the effective school, one that has emphasised the power of the school to make a difference to its students independently of its social and economic conditions. Throughout this time, the educational community has depended on a set of descriptive characteristics that have acted as indicators of success, which, through reform, could be replicated in all schools. It is now time to question whether this basic organisational framework is still the only, or the best, one within which to pursue the goals of universal secondary education. We need to understand the deeper cultural and structural underpinnings of schools that make them effective. I want to use concepts that *explain* why schools are successful not merely *describe* the nature of that success (such a having a culture of achievement, or being well led, and so on). If the same concepts can also be used to explain what makes other kinds of organisation or whole social systems such as cities or societies effective and successful, then the relationship between schools and their wider environment is more explicit. Elsewhere I have set out a conceptual framework to help us understand the capacity of schools to produce excellent educational outcomes as a result of the interaction between different forms of capital. The quality of a school is explained in terms of three concepts – intellectual capital, social capital and organisational capital.

*Intellectual capital* embraces what we usually call human capital, or the education and training of individuals, with allied concepts to cover a broader spectrum – their knowledge, skills, capabilities, competences, talents, expertise, practices and routines. Intellectual capital is one of the invisible assets of an organisation and complements its financial capital and physical assets. Schools are evidently rich in the intellectual capital of the teachers and staff, but also of the students, their families and communities. The capacity of a school to mobilise its intellectual capital is critical, for this is what fosters new ideas and creates new knowledge, which leads to successful innovation in making the school more effective. Such innovation creates new professional practices so that teachers work smarter, not harder.

A second element of a school's invisible assets is its *social capital*, which has both cultural and structural aspects. Culturally, social capital consists in the *trust* that exists between the school's members and its various stakeholders; structurally, social capital is the extent and quality of the *networks* among its members – between head and staff, staff and students, staff and parents – as well as the school's networks with external partners. A school that is rich in social capital has a strong sense of itself as a community, with ties to other communities. Such a school understands the importance of knowledge-sharing. In the most effective schools, the best professional practices – which are of course a form of intellectual capital – are not locked within the minds of a few outstanding teachers and restricted to the privacy of their classrooms, but are the common property of all who might profit from them.

*Organisational capital* refers to the knowledge and skill about how to improve the school by making better use of its intellectual and social capital, especially to enhance teaching and learning. Great school leaders have organisational capital in abundance. They know not only how to deploy the school's existing intellectual and social capital, but also how to increase them. On this view, the primary function of a head is to ensure that as many people as possible have been given leadership opportunities to increase and mobilise the school's intellectual and social capital. Ideally, the school's management and organisational structures should reflect the optimal distribution of these opportunities to contribute to its overall effectiveness, and to learn from what it already does well.

Using the terms intellectual, social and organisational capital provides us with a way of reading across from schools to the community, so that we see how the same underlying forces characterise good schools and good communities (which include many other schools) and that the two are interdependent. As long as we use very different terms for explaining good schools and good communities, we risk talking about how schools can be improved or transformed as if this could be done independently of the community. This is in defiance of the facts and it can generate inflated expectations of what individual school leaders can achieve alone. If intellectual and social capital can be affected by what we choose to do, both in the community and in the school, then there are good grounds for optimism and potential recipes for social improvement, even transformation.

In the following sections, I show how a disciplined approach to creating and using intellectual, social and organisational capital, drawing on knowledge and resources both within and beyond the school, could form the basis of the new strategies that are needed to achieve successful reform in a more diverse and complex environment.

# 4. Transformation through innovation

I agree with Tony Blair that it is impossible to speak of transformation without the concept of innovation. In the world of business and industry, innovation is conventionally defined as 'the exploitation of a new idea that through practical action adds value to a product, process or service'. The reference to processes and services is important, since too great an emphasis on product innovation leads educationalists to think that there is nothing the education service can learn from business, since we do not have an equivalent product. But business is well experienced in innovative processes and services from which education can learn. In education most innovation is the creation of new professional knowledge.

Peter Drucker, the doyen of management gurus, defines innovation as *a change that creates a new dimension of performance.* This definition will be more appealing to ministers and their officials than to practitioners in schools, since it emphasises the outcome rather than the process of education, though the performance might apply to what teachers do, not just what students achieve. The most simple definition of all in the field of education is that innovation or knowledge creation means that practitioners *learn to do things differently in order to do them better.*

Transformation is a big word, one that implies a profound change grounded in some radical (or discontinuous) innovation, not just incremental innovation. In Figure 1, the difference is explained in relation to what teachers do. There are two dimensions: the vertical axis refers to change that is either near to or far from teachers' current

**Figure 1  The nature of innovation**

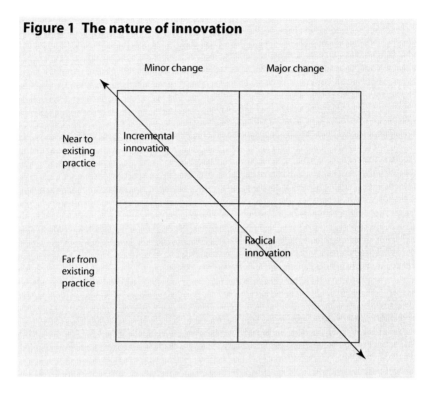

professional practices; the horizontal axis refers to the extent of the change. Incremental innovation is a minor change that is close to existing practice, and radical innovation is a major change that is far from existing practice. Each axis can be seen as a continuum, so that the diagonal can be treated as a kind of innovation scale, going from small, incremental innovations in the top left corner to huge, radical innovations in the bottom right corner.

There are also different types of innovation. We often think of innovation as essentially technological. Some of these technological innovations are truly radical, such as television, the jet engine, the personal computer or more recently the mobile telephone. Radical innovations are often preceded and then followed by incremental innovation. This is clearly the case with the mobile telephone. Though resisted in its earliest conception, its arrival and widespread acceptance has been followed by a vast number of far less significant incremental innovations to retain and increase each firm's position in the market. Often the technology follows a breakthrough in the underlying science: biotechnology and pharmaceuticals frequently depend on advances in 'pure' science. But there are radical innovations that differ substantially from those of a scientific–technological kind. The development in medicine of the randomised controlled trial, which (to many people's surprise) only really gained acceptance after the trial of streptomycin to treat pulmonary tuberculosis in the 1940s, was certainly a radical innovation for it quickly became the gold standard by which the clinical effectiveness of new developments is judged. Yet no technology is involved here: it is a radical innovation in professional methodology. Other radical innovations consist of an importation of what is widely accepted in one field but is radical in another: the steam engine was used in mines for 75 years before it was imported by another industry and adapted to propel boats. Here the radical innovation consisted of the novel application in a different field of a much older idea. Importation as a type of innovation is not unlike the xenograft in medicine: there will be considerable resistance to the transfer – 'Not invented here' and 'Ah, but we're different.'

In the business world many firms in all sectors have gone through deep organisational changes over recent decades. They are very unlike the companies of 50 or 100 years ago. So radical innovation in education might mean a very different kind of organisation for the school. But most schools are surprisingly similar to the schools created by the industrial revolution. At that stage it was the function of state schools to prepare the newly urbanised children for their future life in the factory and so the parallels between the organisation of schools and the organisation of factories were strong. The school may be ripe for radical workplace redesign; one option would be to examine the most impressive of today's workplaces and then redesign schools to serve as a preparation for life in the companies of tomorrow's knowledge economy.

Radical innovation might entail fundamentally new approaches to what goes on in schools. *The London Challenge* offers an agenda:

> We want to free schools to innovate, taking advantage of the nationwide deregulation of the system and new legislative freedoms. The length of the school day, the type of lessons, the patterns of the timetable, partnerships with business, the involvement of parents, the ethos of the schools, the recruitment and retention of teachers, ways of making good behaviour the norm and bad behaviour unacceptable, use of classroom assistants, the shape of the curriculum – all these are ready for reform school by school.[7]

A more radical reform of curriculum and assessment might also be in order. The current secondary curriculum is seen by many to be seriously out of step with the demands of employment in knowledge economies, where new knowledge, skills and attitudes are at a premium – the ability to learn how to learn and other meta-cognitive or 'thinking' skills; the ability to learn on the job and in teams; the ability to cope with ambiguous situations and unpredictable problems; the ability to communicate well verbally, not just in writing; and the ability to be creative, innovative and entrepreneurial. To enable teachers to help students to learn in these ways, and so to organise schools, would indeed be transformation. In the knowledge society teachers could with advantage be models of what their students are to become – highly effective and adaptable learners. We are beginning, through the cognitive and neurosciences, to gain new insights into learning, which in turn might affect how teachers teach as well as how schools are organised.

It is widely believed that there is simply too much formal assessment in secondary schools and that the pressure on teachers and students to do well in so many and such frequent tests and examinations is distorting education. It is clear that *assessment for recording*, the levels and grades that serve a variety of functions, is out of balance with *assessment for learning*, a lever for raising achievement; but the latter is being given insufficient priority by government – probably because it was developed through knowledge creation at school level and not as a central 'initiative'. There are signs that the Department and its ministers are willing to adjust the testing regime to reflect some of these concerns, but the steps taken so far do not have the benefit of a coherent system-wide rationale for developing an alternative set of assessment structures and practices equipped to make the best use of school-based innovation.

In curriculum and assessment reforms, the new information and communication technologies (ICTs) will play a key role. Many students are ahead of teachers in terms of ICT skills and ICT confidence; wise teachers readily learn from students who so eagerly grasp the power embedded in these rapidly changing technologies. ICTs will change both what happens in classrooms and how teachers and students relate to one another. The ICTs might in the medium term have an even greater impact on assessment through computer marking of student work, the provision of tests-when-ready, and the use of virtual reality to provide more imaginative assessment tasks.

Figure 2 shows a map of innovations located in a space constructed by type of innovation and the degree of radicalism involved. It is evident that transformation in education would be accomplished by different kinds of knowledge creation of varying degrees of radicalism. Representing innovations in this form is preferable to a list of 'initiatives' since it draws attention the relations between the components in the bigger picture and how they work in combination. Such a transformation of the teaching profession (roles and practices) and institutions (structures and cultures) will not arise spontaneously but has to be engineered by imaginative and courageous policy-makers, who do not choose between incremental and radical innovation but initiate a programme of innovation that is inevitably somewhat messy but needs to be seen as reasonably clear and coherent to stakeholders and the wider public. The more the transformation is characterised by radical innovation, the more disruptive a change it will be – Schumpeter's 'creative destruction' – and so it would

## Figure 2  A map of innovations in education

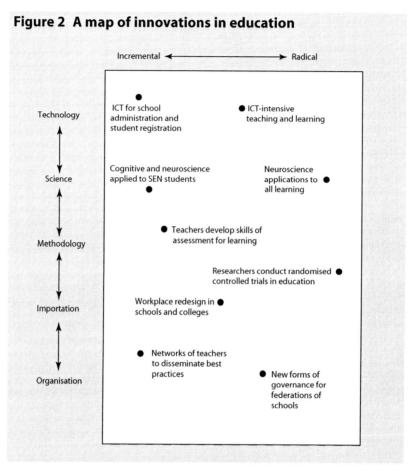

be achieved against considerable resistance, from some teachers, some parents, and some students. That is one of the lessons of the introduction of the literacy and numeracy strategies. A different kind of innovation, the one advocated here, is no less likely to disturb the status quo. The transformation for which ministers seem to call cannot be accomplished either through routine means in a climate of consensus or through further top-down imposition from the centre. A different approach is essential.

# 5. The first transformation – creating the right climate

Innovation is a delicate plant, which thrives in a favourable climate. It grows in stages. It begins with the perception that something needs to change, stimulating the bright ideas about what might be done. Each idea is elaborated and put to an early test, and then either dropped because it proves to be deficient or further supported because it promises to work. Once proved, it is disseminated to those people or places where it can be used to advantage. There are, in short, three key phases in innovation or knowledge creation: the generation of the idea, its application in practice, and its transfer into widespread adoption.

In each phase, innovation can easily be stifled. Each phase, not just the generation of the original idea, requires creativity. Elaborating an idea and subjecting it to test requires another form of creativity, as does knowing how to transfer the newly created knowledge so that it is widely adopted by those who may be wedded to older practices. The process of knowledge creation involves risk-taking: there cannot be innovation that is risk-free. The climate that is most inimical to innovation is a blame culture, which both discourages the creation of new knowledge and undermines the courage needed to take the process through the high-risk phases of application and transfer.

Many people in the education field in England believe that they live in a blame culture. The style of OfSTED inspections, accountability through league tables based on student test performance, and naming and shaming the weakest or 'failing' schools, may have made a positive contribution to school improvement – the issue is much disputed – but without question, when combined with top-down innovations in the form of government 'initiatives', there is in schools a climate of blame, characterised by playing it safe with resentful dependency. Innovation and the associated risk-taking is strangled.

Of course teachers already innovate, and do so constantly. As in all professions that deal with human beings as their raw material, the recipes for handling routine problems can work effectively only when they are implemented in a creative way. Every lesson has its unique features, requiring teachers to devise subtle adaptations to meet the distinctive needs of the students in the class, the nature of the content to be learned, and the classroom atmosphere, which varies widely by time of day and day in the week. Successful teachers know how to adapt their routines to fit the occasion. Over a professional lifetime, teachers work by trial and error to develop this extensive repertoire of skills. Most teachers engage in regular minor experimentation to discover 'what works', but it is, to use Michael Huberman's felicitous term, a case of *tinkering*. Huberman points out that teachers, like artisans, work mainly alone, cobbling together ideas and materials out of which, through repeated tinkering, they devise strategies and routines to make teaching and learning work effectively in variable conditions.[8]

Innovation has not disappeared from English schools over the last 20 years, but it has declined and has tended to go underground, surviving in spite of government policy rather than thriving because of it. Transformation means that such covert, personalised, micro-innovation is no longer adequate to the task facing schools, which will now need to create and sustain an explicit climate of experimentation and planned innovation that characterises business firms, whose very survival depends on successful knowledge creation. For the centre cannot devise enough innovation across the whole range of teacher practices to implement the demanded rate of change. Moreover, the teaching profession will accept only a limited amount of prescription from the centre without loss of professional morale. If teachers are to take ownership of reform through innovation in their practices, they must play a part in their creation.

An essential task for government is to create a climate in which it is possible to promote among teachers:

O the *motivation* to create new professional knowledge
O the *opportunity* to engage actively in innovation
O the *skills* for testing the validity of the new knowledge
O the means for transferring the validated innovations rapidly within their school and into other schools.

This means that government must give active permission to schools to innovate and provide a climate in which failure can be given a different meaning, as a necessary element in making progress, as is the case in the business world (see Box 1). But there is no point in the government giving such permission unless it is accompanied by a restoration of trust in the profession. Without this investment in the system's social capital, risks will be avoided, mistakes will be hidden, and innovation and the associated professional learning will decline. To capitalise on the advantage that trust confers in fostering innovation, fear of failure has to be removed. This means turning mistakes into opportunities for learning: mistakes can be accepted or even encouraged, provided that they are a means to improvement. The government's 'power to

---

**Box 1 Failing towards success in business**

The fastest way to succeed is to double your failure rate.

*Thomas Watson, IBM*

Fail often to succeed sooner.

*Tom Kelley, IDEO*

Be failure tolerant: analyse rather than praise or penalise.

*Jack Welch, GE*

You must learn to fail intelligently. Failing is one of the greatest arts in the world. One fails forward towards success.

*Thomas Edison*

---

innovate', by which schools may apply to the Secretary of State for permission to make changes that might aid teaching and learning, is an important step in the right direction. However, unless it is accompanied by a wider change in climate, it is likely to remain symbolic and under-used.

These lessons have been fully learned in organisations that know how to innovate. One example is the After Action Review (AAR), from the US army. The AAR works with three standard questions that are posed after any major activity in which a perfect performance is unlikely:

○ What was supposed to happen?
○ What did happen?
○ What accounts for the difference?

Identifying the gap between the ideal and the actual, and explaining the gap, aids learning for the future. Hunting for mistakes and then assigning blame inhibits learning. There is a backward *post mortem* aspect, certainly; but it is about tracking the sequence of events and cause–effect relationships so that successes and failures can be unpacked. The overall thrust is to the future – the lessons to be learned so that success can be embedded in future action and failures will not be repeated. The AAR supports doing things differently next time: innovating for improvement. It's a classic case of Edison's failing forward.

Unless schools acquire a willingness to take risks, and to learn from the inevitable mistakes, there can be no real innovation at school level. The blame culture has to be abandoned as an impediment to transformation.

# 6. The second transformation – disciplining innovation

A school that encouraged every member of staff to innovate on any preferred area, and then provided support for the activity, would squander its efforts on ideas that would rarely turn into transferable applications. The essential first step for an innovative school is to avoid innovation overload and excessive diversity by choosing and agreeing upon a limited focus or content for the main innovative activity that can be well managed.

The government is right to strive to free teachers to innovate, both by removing constraints and providing opportunities. The danger is that if teachers do this then every school will create its own agenda for innovation and so unleash a spate of innovation that will run wild in the 1960s spirit of letting a thousand flowers bloom. The result will not be a strong evidence base of how to do things differently to guarantee doing them better. Moreover, even if the new knowledge were sound, there are very weak means for disseminating it to other teachers and schools. It is important that teachers launch a new era of innovation, but it is absolutely essential that the knowledge creation be undertaken in a highly disciplined way.

In the first place, there is little point in innovating on every possible aspect of secondary schooling; we must think through which aspects are most valuable as themes for innovation. Limiting the content means deciding on priorities. This can be done through a professional knowledge audit to clarify what secondary teachers know how to do well and what they do not know or do not do well. Every school has to pose the questions: *what is the most important and urgent problem area and where do we think we could innovate successfully?* This can be achieved when every secondary school explores three questions:

○ What do we need to know to be better equipped in this problem area?

○ What do we currently know about this problem area?

○ What do we need to do to close the gap?

And this can be collated to provide a picture of the overall needs of the secondary sector.

It would, of course, be absurd to attempt to restrict the areas in which any individual school might choose to innovate, but the choice of innovation will be more rational if it is informed by an understanding of the needs of the sector as a whole. It is not innovative schools that we need, but an *innovation system* in which the schools that choose to innovate can have a transformative effect on themselves and potentially on all other secondary schools.

Every school has to decide whether it wants to engage in innovation, on what topics and on what scale. Some will innovate little or not at all, some innovate a lot, and many will innovate a modest amount. Transformation does not require every school to become an innovative school: every school reinventing the wheel would be a prodigious waste of time and energy. A school in 'special measures' will have to attend to basic issues, such as student discipline and class management as well as the basics of literacy and numeracy. A school at the other end of the spectrum may well be resting on its laurels and see little reason to engage in innovation.

The schools most likely to welcome innovation, especially of a radical kind, are those where two conditions can be met. First, their headteachers are convinced that complacency is dangerous and that many things could and should be done better. The government's designation of our 'best' schools as *leading-edge schools* is well chosen and preferable to the term *beacon schools.* Unlike beacons, leading-edge schools are on the move to something better. Secondly, the schools must be ones where teachers can be provided with the necessary opportunities to innovate. Experimentation in pursuit of innovation, as the world of business knows, cannot be done in addition to normal work, but must be embedded in the routine. Each stage of the knowledge creation process takes time: generating new ideas, testing them in application, and transferring the outcomes to all who can profit from them. Innovation doesn't work when teachers feel overworked, jaded and neglected, or if they are not recognised or rewarded for it.

If leading-edge schools – by definition a minority – take the lead in knowledge creation, what happens to innovation in the rest of the system? Transformation is achieved in two ways: by moving the best schools (or departments within them) further ahead and by closing the gap between the least and most effective schools (or subject departments). Transformation combines 'moving ahead' with 'levelling up'. In effect there are two forms of innovation in the education service. The first is *front-line innovation* conducted by leading-edge institutions and government-supported 'pathfinders', which develop new ideas into original practices.

The second kind of innovation, 'levelling up', entails the weakest schools 'catching up' with what better schools already do. When a school in difficulty adopts practices that are well established in other schools, the change represents an innovation for the staff involved; what is 'old hat' to high-performing schools may seem dramatically new and different to those struggling against the odds. This learning from others, this adoption of second-hand practices, might be called *transferred innovation*. Hitherto the most common mechanisms for achieving transferred innovation have been somewhat indirect. A low-performing school is required to produce an action plan for its improvement, but the means of achieving transferred innovation is rarely explicit. In extreme cases a new headteacher is brought in to 'turn the school round'. This is *transferred leadership*, which undoubtedly leads to the importation of some new practices, especially where the head appoints new staff, who become direct bearers of transferred innovation.

Since highly innovative schools will be in a minority, transformation depends crucially on the capacity of the system to manage transferred innovation. This will be best achieved where schools are bound into close collaborative relationships with one another or, as we shall see, embedded in networks, especially groups of schools that are beginning to develop federations or collegiates. Because a federation is so much larger than an individual school, it can prioritise a shared topic for knowledge creation and have a much more sophisticated design, both for sharing the innovative workload, so each school undertakes a limited and variable amount of activity, and for testing it more rigorously than is ever possible in a single secondary school or department. Many secondary schools are too small to undertake the development or testing of innovation. Federations offer the increased size so that cross-school collaboration can generate strong innovation. There are several options here.

○ Several schools might test different solutions to a common problem, to check which solutions are most effective.
○ Several schools might test the same innovation, but do so in contrasting circumstances to check if the innovation works in spite of such differences.
○ Several specialist schools of the same specialism might take different aspects of a common innovation, so that at a later stage each school contributes one element of an overall innovation that would have been too large for a single school to test.
○ Several schools agree to engage in a randomised controlled trial on a problem that needs to be solved but at present there is no reason to prefer one solution over another.

Options such as these would generate a far more robust evidence base for an innovation in a far shorter time than leaving knowledge creation to the idiosyncratic preferences and limited resources of a single institution. Recent developments in school-based research, such as the Best Practice Research Scholarships and research consortia among schools, must evolve within this new discipline if they are to survive.

In schools that are centres of innovation the tasks of school leaders change, for hitherto schools have not seen knowledge creation as one of their central purposes. Where innovation has taken place, it has been an optional extra for individuals or small teams with a particular interest in such developmental work. There has been little time for it, especially as professional training days have increasingly been taken over by the need to respond to initiatives from the centre. And the inspection framework gives no credit for innovation, even though it often lies behind the exceptional performance that is itself recognised.

The first element in leadership for innovation will be not so much 'the management of change', which is adequate when the reforms are externally imposed and their acceptance and implementation have to be legitimised and managed at school level by headteachers. Knowledge creation needs a culture of experimentation with a philosophy of 'lessons learned' embodied in a leader who 'walks the talk' by being a risk-taker who admits to making mistakes. Innovative schools require leaders to exploit the school's own assets and innovative capacities.

The most effective leaders are likely to have the qualities of what Jim Collins calls 'Level Five' leaders.[9] Collins selected companies that had achieved not just short-term success, but rather an exceptional level of success over a sustained period. Their leaders were not simply good, but great. It is striking that these leaders did not fit the tough, high-profile, charismatic image in which they are portrayed in the popular media. They were modest, reserved and understated rather than dazzling, larger-than-life heroes with gargantuan egos. At the same time, they had a deep, passionate and wilful commitment to achieve clear goals for their organisation. Level Five leaders:

O   are ambitious for their organisation, not for themselves
O   talk about their organisation, not about themselves
O   have a dogged, unwavering, ferocious resolve
O   are fanatically driven with an incurable need to produce

sustained results
- ○ are more like plough horses than show horses
- ○ apportion credit to events outside themselves when things go well
- ○ take personal responsibility when things go badly
- ○ set up their successors for even greater success.

When English headteachers are being appointed, they are expected by the governing body to articulate a clear vision for the school, which they promise they will implement if appointed. Level Five leaders, by contrast, do not set a new vision. Instead they select the right people for the senior positions and then agree collectively the direction for the company. As Collins puts it, Level Five leaders get the right people on the bus, and the wrong people off the bus, and then figure out where to drive it. The head of an innovative school recruits senior colleagues with the right intellectual and social capital and then channels these powerful assets towards the achievement of a jointly defined mission.

Significantly, very few Level Five leaders were appointed from outside the company, whereas among school headteachers it is more common to appoint from outside than inside. We may have it wrong in education in assuming that 'fresh blood at the top' is a lever of school improvement. While this may apply to schools that are (close to) failing, it may need an insider to take a good school to greatness because they build on what they inherit rather than striving towards a different vision against the inclinations and preferences of the staff. An insider may have a better grasp of the school's weaknesses and is thus able to face the facts brutally and so do something about them – innovate.

The headteacher's attitude to the new technologies is crucial. Level Five leaders invest in ICTs; but they do not use them as the primary means of igniting a transformation. They do not incorporate all the latest gadgets and follow the various fads and fashions of the ICT market. Rather, they select their ICTs very carefully to fit and advance the core mission of the company. As Collins explains, they use ICTs to accelerate, not to create, the momentum of transformation. In the case of schools, this would be to improve administration and assessment as well as teaching and learning. Classroom teachers do not want to become experts in the use of ICT, and most are not interested in improving their ICT skills in a general way; instead, they want to be expert teachers of physics or French, mathematics or music, and if ICTs will help them teach these subjects better, they will use them for this overriding purpose, which is at the heart of transformation.

Forging the culture of highly disciplined innovation for transformation requires governments to become skilful brokers of relationships among the stakeholders in education, so that schools have the confidence to engage in the necessary experimentation and the public can be persuaded both to consent to experiments in education for the common good, as they have in the case of medicine, and to accept that education cannot be free of risk and failure if rapid progress is to be made. This is a delicate task, which only governments can undertake and without which education (and perhaps other public services) will continue to lag behind the pace of change in the private sector. Transformation means a much more explicit commitment to and support for front-line innovation, combined with a massive enhancement of transferred innovation so that it works more effectively than at present on the weakest schools but also works for schools in the 'middle' range. This requires *a new strategy for the lateral transfer of innovation.*

# 7. The third transformation – devising and implementing a lateral strategy

Transferred innovation is a simple idea, but moving knowledge is a difficult practice. It will not work unless we have a clear and shared picture of what is 'good practice' in education – and especially in teaching and learning and in institutional leadership – and how this knowledge and skill can be further developed and transferred rapidly round a large system of some 25,000 schools and around half a million staff.

Much is written about the 'the sharing of good practice' and 'the dissemination of best practice': documents published by the DfES and its associated authorities and agencies gush with this rhetoric. Unfortunately our knowledge of how this might best be done is frighteningly slight. Where it is being done, it is not necessarily being done particularly well or as a result of official action. The explanation for this state of affairs lies in our superficial knowledge of what most practitioners – mainly headteachers and teachers – actually do in schools.

O  Most teachers work alone in classrooms for most of the time: one teacher with a group of students. It is not usual for them to work together with students or to be observed by other teachers. So much of the detail of what teachers actually do – their professional practices of how they manage their students and teach their subject – is largely hidden.

○ The judgement that a teacher's practice is good derives less from direct observation than from his or her reputation among peers, which is based on evidence such as test and examination results and the judgements of inspectors, as well as on how the teacher is treated by students in public places.

○ Every institution has its own knowledge about its strengths and weaknesses. This is gained through a school's internal *self-assessment*, though this has only recently been resuscitated after years of excessive reliance on external review. OfSTED inspections may well validate internal review as well as complement it. But these assessments of quality are stated in broad-brush terms that rarely catch the fine detail of teacher practices. A committed teacher who reads the OfSTED report on a highly successful school is simply not given sufficient information to be able to replicate in a new context more than a few of the praised practices.

○ It is difficult for most schools to judge how they fare against current 'good' or 'best' practice, since they have relatively superficial knowledge of what is done in other institutions. Today there are better sources of comparative data available to educational leaders than ever before, such as value-added or benchmarked data on student achievement and OfSTED reports providing a scrutiny of a far wider canvas of the institution. Yet even inspectorial judgements of what constitutes 'good practice' are by no means always based on explicit criteria. These judgements may be trustworthy, but they do not necessarily clarify the implied *scale* of any practice that varies from poor to good and, presumably, to the top of the scale that would constitute 'best practice'. OfSTED reports may tell us whether an inspected establishment has improved since its last inspection, and whether such reports, when aggregated, signify a country-wide improvement among schools. But they are much weaker at what must be a central task of educational transformation, namely *the precise definition and identification of what can be shown to be best practice.*

In short, much that is said about 'good practice' is based on mere opinion or unsubstantiated assertion rather than robust evidence about 'what works' in particular circumstances.

An effective lateral strategy for transferred innovation has several components, each of which tackles a strategic element that is currently neglected in government policy. It must become clear what is meant by 'good' and 'best' practice among teachers; there needs to be a method of locating good practices and sound innovations; innovations must be ones that bring real advantages to teachers; and methods of transferring innovation effectively have to be devised.

### 'Good' practice and 'best' practice are rigorously defined

What is meant by 'good practice'? Sometimes it refers to standard practices that are considered effective, part of a profession's repertoire or 'custom and practice'. Novices are expected to learn these. Sometimes the term refers to a less common or recently devised practice that is thought to be better or more effective than the standard; many innovations fall into this category, especially when they remain untested but are advocated by their creators. However, greater effectiveness is not necessarily more efficient. For example, a new practice for the teacher may help a student learn better, but the cost to the teacher, in terms of time or energy, may be so great that the costs of the new practice outweigh the benefits. For a practice to be a good one it should have *high leverage,* that is, it should have a large effect for a small energy input. A new practice of low leverage, where the energy input is disproportionate to the outcome achieved, hardly qualifies as 'good practice'. High leverage is the key to teachers working smarter, not harder, and should be at the heart of transferred innovation.

A second consideration is how easily a practice is transferable from one person or setting to another. As we shall examine later, some practices are much more transferable than others. Thus a practice that is very difficult to transfer tends to be confined to a small number of people in a restricted range of circumstances, and is not in general terms a good practice of wider value to the profession. What works for a primary school teacher may not work for a sixth-form teacher; what works in a rural area may not transfer to an inner-city school. A good practice is one that is easily transferred to many other practitioners and to many other settings.

Often 'good practice' and 'best practice' are treated as synonyms, though clearly 'best practice' suggests a practice that has been compared with others and has proved itself better than other 'good practices'. Again, a best practice might be more effective than others at achieving its purpose; but its value is limited if it is of low leverage and low transferability. *The best practices that are of most interest are the ones that work but are also of high leverage and easily transferable.* Innovation has to be highly disciplined if good practices are to evolve by a process akin to natural selection into best practices.

In summary, transferred innovation in education depends on a rigorous definition of professional best practices, namely practices that work, but with the important additional benefits of high leverage and high transferability. Otherwise, there is a danger of wasting much time and effort on seeking to disseminate practices that are of little proven worth and are in any event difficult to move from their innovative source.

## Innovations and best practice are identified

To achieve transferred innovation, priorities would have to be determined, since not all areas could be tackled immediately. A systematic search *from all possible sources* of existing practices in the priority areas considered to be good or innovative would then be initiated. This is not as simple as it might seem, for there is much good practice within the system but often it is in effect hidden, locked in the minds of individuals or inside the boundaries of the insulated classroom or school. OfSTED and Her Majesty's Inspectorate evidence and experience would be crucial here, as would the knowledge of subject associations, teacher trainers and LEA advisers. This would yield a pool of potential good and best practice in each priority area. It is likely that no more than some 20 per cent of practices would be judged as potentially good.

## Best practices are highly leveraged and 'teacher-friendly'

Much of the good practice, whether existing or emerging through knowledge creation, cannot be imposed on the workforce, as was in effect the case with literacy and numeracy; practitioners will have to *choose* to adopt the practices. People often reject (choose not to entertain) new practices in the form of central 'initiatives', which are often seen as a burden rather than a support, and in the government's interest rather than the interest of practitioners or students. Teachers have become suspicious of new ideas flowing from the centre, and this caution has been interpreted as resistance to change. In truth, teachers willingly accept new practices that are teacher-friendly, that make their lives better or easier in some way. Teachers do not mind doing something that is unfamiliar and difficult, provided that they can see some real benefit to students and that the effort demanded is not unreasonable. It is therefore essential that the most significant of the good practices identified will be those that are of 'high leverage'.

It is additionally advantageous if a set of good practices in a particular area can be scrutinised to determine which of the set is indeed the best practice, namely the one that is of the highest leverage and can be transferred to other practitioners most readily. This would take time to determine, and would require investigation by teacher researchers as well as professional researchers. By these stringent criteria, the emergent best practices would be relatively small in number and could be the focus of a major campaign of innovation transfer, as should be the case with assessment for learning.[10]

## Champions of innovation and best practice are identified

Innovations and best practices do not spread naturally or easily, either in the world of business or in education. The present methods of knowledge transfer used by DfES, and indeed by many who are professionally engaged in educational research and development, rely on the written documentation of good practice, and more recently on websites, videos, and so on. And many practitioners adopt much the same methods: a school can advertise itself as well as aim to offer practical suggestions to others through a website. These methods of knowledge transfer are easy for officials and developers to devise or commission, but research has shown them to be weak mechanisms for disseminating new practices. New practices are not likely to spread very far or very quickly if they are advocated by the DfES in a glossy booklet or academic publication sent to every school – as both will remain unread by the majority – or by a school's website, which is largely unseen (unless it is known to be a demonstrated way of improving the school's league table position). Even if these sources were read or seen, the extent of knowledge transfer would be very limited for a simple reason: it is very hard to transfer knowledge that is disembodied and decontextualised.

The best way to spread new practices that people must choose voluntarily rather than conform to in response to central prescription is *through peers*. Innovations have to catch on, like best-selling books, because they seem to be what everybody is doing, or are caught from personal contact, like a virus. The irony here is that the DfES has an extremely valuable infrastructure – the regular posting of materials to every school in the country – but the content of its messages lacks credibility with practitioners. When schools want to send news of innovations to other schools, they have the credibility but not the right infrastructure, since combing through thousands of websites or reading teacher-authored articles scattered around many magazines are inefficient ways of discovering good practices. What is needed is innovation news that is credible and an infrastructure by means of which the news can travel far and quickly.

It is essential to identify 'champions' of the identified good or best practices, who will have an authority and credibility that DfES officials or academics can rarely achieve. Champions are of two kinds.

Practitioner-champions, who have devised and successfully applied the innovation with known beneficial outcomes, are the most important. Alongside them are advocate-champions, who have some authority in the field, for instance an LEA adviser, a researcher who has helped to evaluate the innovation, or simply a well-known and trusted person.

Champions will need to be rewarded and recognised for doing the work – and so will their host schools, colleges or workplaces, since they will need to spend time on it. Knowledge transfer among teachers is often difficult to achieve. Although the idea behind an innovation is easy to describe, the way in which it is implemented or applied in practice often depends on tacit knowledge – the kind of knowledge that is hard to put into words, such as the knowledge of how to ride a bicycle. So *best practice has to be demonstrated*, not just explained, and its replication by another practitioner in somewhat different circumstances has to be practised through trial and error; this entails *creatively adapting* the innovation that is being transferred. The donor and the recipient in the transfer process need to spend some time together if the transfer is to be successful, since just as the donor had to engage in learning to develop the innovation, so too must the recipient learn during the transfer. What now seems simple to the experienced innovator is likely to seem complicated to the novice. All this takes time, both for the donor to offer the necessary mentoring, coaching and shadowing, and for the recipient to make the necessary adjustments so that the innovation works in its new setting. The innovation transfer works when the knowledge involved remains embodied and contextualised in a working relationship that is co-creative for both participants.

Eric von Hippel created the term 'sticky' to describe information that is difficult to transfer from one person to another. The idea is that information does not simply slip unimpeded down some communication channel between donor and recipient, but may stick in varying degrees on its journey: the greater the stickiness, the less successful the transfer.[11] Stickiness can be located in the donor (a reluctance to share), in the channel of communication (a poor explanation of the innovation), or in the recipient (not identifying with the donor's problem that the innovation solves). Gabriel Szulanski has offered hypotheses about the factors that may increase stickiness in the transfer of an innovation or best practice.[12] So stickiness increases when:

○ it is not clear exactly how and why the new practice works
○ the donor is not motivated to share fully
○ the donor is not credible in the eyes of the recipient
○ the recipient is not motivated to accept the innovation ('not invented here')
○ the recipient's organisation is barren ground for new ideas
○ the relationship between donor and recipient lacks respect and intimacy.

All these are suggestive 'dos and don'ts' for transferred innovation in education. The successful transfer of innovation takes time; but this cost has to be weighed against the huge amount of time and energy that is currently lavished on transfer that simply does not work. *We need to replace weak means of transferring large numbers of untested, so-called good practices, with a strong means of transferring small numbers of robust best practices.*

## Transferring innovations and best practices though networks

Effective champions are practitioners who are well connected to other practitioners and have the skills to 'sell' a good practice and offer practical support to peers who are willing to adopt it, but need help to do so. Champions should therefore be sought in leading-edge schools, where they are most likely to be embedded in structures that aid dissemination. Champions have personal networks of friends and colleagues, and may well include LEA or LLSC networks and professional networks such as subject associations, the Specialist Schools Trust, the British Educational Communications and Technology Agency (Becta), Excellence in Cities, consortia, collegiates and federations. The networked learning communities of the National College for School Leadership could be especially valuable here.

Indeed, it is arguable that these bodies are crucial hubs in a networked school system and that one of the main purposes of LEAs, many of which are currently on the defensive and confused about their role, is to encourage and support networks of practitioners.

Not all practitioner-champions are locked into large networks or have the skills to transfer their practices; there are innovators who are modest and reticent about what they have learned to do well. Advocate-champions are opinion leaders, people of influence, and so are embedded in larger networks; they are the mediators who link the less entrepreneurial practitioner-champions to others to bridge the process of innovation transfer.

A school or practitioner who creates the knowledge behind a powerful innovation faces four options over what to do with it. They are:

O keep it to yourself
O sell it for profit
O share it with a partner
O give it away for free to anybody who wants it.

In a highly competitive climate, the pressure on a school staff is to keep successful innovations to themselves in order to maintain their competitive edge, that is, position in the league tables and popularity among parents. Why give away one's best ideas? If they have to be given away, if only because they might well leak away or be stolen, it is sensible to sell them. One school is said to have made over a million pounds by selling an IT course that has helped 100 per cent of its own students to achieve five A*–C grades at GCSE. But neither of these provides a path to transformation, which requires schools that are rich in best practice to share or exchange their innovations or give them away for free.

Exchanging innovations is an attractive proposition because of the deeply embedded 'norm of reciprocity' by which if I give you something you feel obliged to return something of equal value, so we both gain. If I give you more than you give me, the relationship is not necessarily destroyed, since in return you may offer me respect for my superiority, so I get a compensatory status boost in return for my asymmetrical gifts to you. But when applied to schools, the norm of reciprocity could mean that the more effective schools would be inclined to exchange best practice with other above average schools, which would simply widen the gap between the best and worst schools, and thus not contribute to system transformation. Moreover, a partnership between two schools is most likely to prosper in a relationship of 'mutual growth', each giving something to the other, but a school seeking rapid development needs access to good practices far beyond the deep partnerships between schools, which are inevitably small in number.

The path to transformation requires every school to be willing to give away its innovations for free, perhaps in the hope of some return, but with no guarantee of it. Is there an example of how this might work? Yes. It is the culture that characterised the beginnings of the internet, which itself started out as a peer-to-peer network of cooperating users. Its original conception and design in the late 1960s was to share computing resources between several American academic centres as equals, each of whom acted as both server and client. In the same way, Tim Berners-Lee, working at CERN, designed the origins of what became the Web as a way for physicists to share research data.[13] During the internet's commercialisation, this early symmetry was lost as huge numbers of clients came to be handled by a small number of branded servers, and many passive consumers became dependent on a few commercial producers. Today many want to restore aspects of the earlier decentralised model to enhance peer-to-peer networks and the norms of sharing in the 'hacker culture' (see Box 2).

Hackers are not the secretive, lone criminals who break into other people's computers with malicious intent as presented in the media – these people are properly called 'crackers'. Rather, hackers are passionate innovators, the expert programmers and networking wizards who, through cooperation and free communication, played the pivotal role in the creation of the internet. The overarching goal of the culture is performance and technological excellence, because this is what determines the common need for sharing and for keeping

## Box 2  The hacker culture

A theorem for life in simple formula: $H = F3$ or happiness equals food, fun and friends.

*Steve Wozniak, who built the first personal computer*

That is how something like Linux comes about. You don't worry about making that much money. The reason that Linux hackers do something is that they find it to be very interesting, and they like to share this interesting thing with others. Suddenly, you both get entertainment from the fact that you are doing something interesting, and you also get the social part. This is how you have this fundamental Linux networking effect where you have a lot of hackers working together because they enjoy what they do. Hackers believe there is no higher stage of motivation than that.

*Linus Tovalds, original creator of Linux*

The Web is more a social creation than a technical one. I designed it for a social effect – to help people work together – and not as a technical toy. The ultimate goal of the Web is to support and improve our weblike existence in the world.

*Tim Berners-Lee, creator of the World Wide Web*

[T]he regulations within which the network lives are increasingly shifting power away from the innovators and toward those who would stifle innovation ... This battle is about who[se] vision of creativity ... should control the future of ideas ... The forces that the original Internet threatened to transform are well on their way to transforming the Internet.

*Lawrence Lessig*

the source code open. A paramount value is freedom – to create, to appropriate whatever is available, and to redistribute the knowledge. Each contribution to software development is posted on the internet in the expectation of reciprocity. The inner joy of creation is a source of satisfaction as is achieving recognition within the community of practice. Like professional scientists, hackers commit themselves to openness, to replicability and peer review, with due credit to those who make significant advances. Hackers have little interest in financial gain through selling their ideas. Instead, they are committed to common ownership of their collective productions.

A classic example here is Linus Torvalds, who in 1991 as a 22-year-old student at the University of Helsinki set out to create a free operating system, and involved others from the beginning by asking them for their ideas, which were then shared within the emerging network. Anybody could contribute and anybody was free to use the improved outcomes. The result was the rapid emergence of the new system, Linux, and its creative development through collaboration at an astonishing rate. Many thousands of users have devoted time and energy to testing and improving Linux, so much so that it has become a threat to Microsoft's Windows – no mean achievement.

Torvalds's ingenuity, which is not technical but sociological in the developmental model that produced Linux, has been captured by Eric Raymond's contrast between the cathedral and the bazaar.[14] Before Torvalds, a software project of this scope was understood to be similar to the construction of a cathedral: many individual craftsmen working slowly to construct the grand design. Linux, by contrast, was constructed at an incredibly fast pace by a community resembling a babbling bazaar of different agendas and approaches and consisting of many users who were recruited as fellow builders – another version of our earlier story of innovation being driven by users. It did not fall apart, but worked brilliantly, to the astonishment of those who were used to, and comfortable with, cathedrals. For Linux should have conformed to Brooks's Law (see Box 3), which predicts that thousands of programmers trying to build a new operating system merely produce an unstable mess; but it did not.

Could something similar happen in education? Could we complement the cathedral of the literacy, numeracy and Key Stage 3 strategies with bazaars of complementary strategies for innovation and its

**Box 3  Brooks's Law**

Fred Brooks's Law states that as the number of programmers $n$ rises, work performed by them rises at the same rate, but complexity and vulnerability to bugs rises as $n$ squared. A corollary of the law is that adding more programmers to a late project makes it later still.

transfer? Could this work and not become an innovation Tower of Babel? Could this aid and accelerate the process of transformation?

A key to transformation is for the teaching profession to establish innovation networks that capture the spirit and culture of internet hackers – the passion, the can-do, the collective sharing. Teachers could create an 'innovation commons' for education, in parallel to the digital commons of the open source movement, a common pool of resources to which innovators contribute and on which any school or teacher might draw to improve professional practice. This could be a professionally self-governing, decentralised means of supporting both front-line and transferred innovation that needs no central control. An innovation commons could be self-sustaining in that those who draw on the common resources make a return to the pool for the benefit they have gained. It is not a matter of a direct or specific exchange between two teachers or schools, but a generalised exchange through the creation of a pool. As Peter Kollock has argued, if I help a stranded motorist who is a stranger, I do not expect this person to return the favour to me, but I hope that if I am ever in a similar situation, some third person will offer to help me.[15] This requires an initial generosity and the taking of a risk that I might never get a return. In effect, contributors to the pool would be offering their innovations and best practices as public goods in the confidence of creating an educational equivalent to the Linux phenomenon.

Success depends on two factors. First, the innovations or best practices being offered are not just 'bright ideas' but practices that have been shown to work and yet are capable of further development.

Secondly, they are practices that are highly relevant and central to what other teachers do in their jobs, that is, not something that might be used on rare occasions. If these two conditions are not met, then the costs and risks of transferring the new practice may well outweigh its possible benefits. But if they are met then the costs of making a generalised reciprocation may also be low, in forms such as:

○ a report on how they made, or failed to make, a successful transfer of the innovation to their own circumstances in the spirit of 'lessons learned' from which others might profit
○ a documented modification of, or advance upon, the original innovation.

These would in both cases be shared, as in Linux, with anybody on the commons with an interest and who might potentially contribute to the next round of lessons learned or usable advances. The disadvantage of cathedral-type strategies, such as literacy and numeracy, is that, despite being evidence-informed in their construction, there is a risk that they become frozen as 'best practice' rather than continually evolving as a result of practitioner innovation. Moreover, there are always academic and practitioner critics ready to point to weaknesses, thus throwing the centre on the defensive. The advantage of bazaar-based strategies is that this same gauntlet is thrown out to the critics: come up with a better idea and prove it is an advance (including increasing the leverage level for teachers), and there is no good reason not to make an emergent 'best practice' widely available to users.

A hacker, said Eric Raymond, is 'an enthusiast, an artist, a tinkerer, a problem solver, and expert'[16] – terms that will arouse fellow feeling in any classroom teacher. For years the profession has complained that government education policy has *reduced teachers to technicians*, rather than respecting them as creative professionals. Ironically, the hacker culture that produced innovative technologies displays values and norms that are quite close to those of teachers, who must now introduce into the education service the very practices that allowed the hackers to transform their world through creative collaboration.

# 8. The fourth transformation – using ICT laterally

Why are the new technologies so important here? What contribution has ICT to make to transformation? The huge potential of the new technologies as an important part of the infrastructure for innovation networks has yet to be realised.

In an education system that consists of schools linked to one another in networks in which schools that are sources of best practice become nodes, it should be relatively simple for a school or teacher to get in touch with a peer as a source of best practice, as a centre of innovation, or as a partner – and in *any* area of educational concern. This capacity is because of the power of *six degrees of separation.*

Nearly 30 years ago, an American social psychologist, Stanley Milgram, performed a startling experiment to demonstrate our inter-connectivity. To investigate the separation between any two people in the USA, he explored how many acquaintances were needed to connect any two randomly selected people. The first person, the sender, was asked to try to get a letter to a named stranger, the target, in a distant town but without an address, by sending it to somebody known to the sender who might actually know the target person or might know somebody better able to reach the target. The question was this: how many persons might intervene before the letter actually reached its destination and how long might it take? The surprising answer was that in most cases between five and six intermediaries were needed, taking a relatively short time. This result gave birth to the notion that we humans are divided by just 'six degrees of separation'. How is this amazing result, this small world, possible? Put mathematically, how could billions of dots be joined in such a way that one could connect any two dots by travelling along just six of the linking lines? The answer, of course, requires us to understand the architecture of networks, which has become a science in itself. In practice, in most real world network structures, the degrees of separation are small.

ICT potentially provides a network structure to turn thousands of secondary schools and their teachers into another small world, in which any two nodes can connect with one another easily and quickly, for without this an attempted transformation through transferred innovation is too shallow and too slow. Given the right infrastructure, a teacher or school wanting to target a peer who might know about or be interested in a particular professional practice, the chances are that by asking someone they know to check among people they know, the chain to the right peer would be very short. Innovation networks supported by ICT could turn secondary schools into the small world that makes transformation possible.

Of course, a teacher could simply advertise a need or interest in the *Times Educational Supplement* or on a website and hope that somebody out there might respond. But network tracking would almost always give a better and faster result and could have the advantage that the responding person or institution would have the pleasure of being approached through a friend's recommendation, one of the best routes into cooperation. Moreover, the process of tracking along the chain might well be an introduction into a network or community of practice that might otherwise go quite undiscovered.

It works the other way round, too. Many of the government's educational agencies – the Qualifications and Curriculum Authority, the British Educational and Communications and Technology Agency, the Teacher Training Agency – are existing hubs. If innovative schools also become hubs in the network, they have an outward flow to a large number of nodes, many of which can help in the process of transfer. It is known that knowledge transfer is often best carried out not by the outstanding expert but by the person who has recently implemented the new practice and is therefore most familiar with the obstacles to transfer, the 'stickiness' that must be overcome through adaptation and learning during the transfer process. Innovating hubs could develop satellites, or acolytes, representing the first cohort to whom an innovation or best practice is successfully transferred. The satellites would take the pressure off potentially over-stretched hubs, thus spreading the load of transferred innovation. The task of government here would be to support the system so that enough hubs and satellites are created to allow transferred innovation to spread through the system without breaking the back of the innovative hubs. For example, government might provide the resources by which champions in innovative hubs trained champions from satellites to work on the next tier as well as providing necessary protection for the innovative hubs.

At the same time, we should not underestimate the capacity of innovation and best practice networks to devise solutions to problems that arise, or to borrow ideas from the net. Take the way Amazon.com works, for instance. You look up a topic, and are provided with a list of books. You look up a book and in addition to details of its content, price, and so on, two further resources are put at your disposal. First, you are offered reviews of the books, by the author or professional reviewers, as well as other Amazon customers. You are also told whether customers found these reviews helpful. Secondly, Amazon tells you which other books a purchaser of the target book has also bought. Displayed before you is an elaborate set of factual information and evaluations to help you make a more informed decision about book-buying.

Epinions.com offers a similar service. It will search millions of products and services – books, movies, cars, restaurants, computers, sports, travel, and so on – and tell you where to get the lowest price for them and which stores are most trusted by customers. Products and services are reviewed and rated by customers, and these are available to all other customers. Customers rate reviewers for the quality of their reviews, and reviewers whose judgements are trusted by their peers are designated top reviewers. You are also told which other reviewers the top reviewers most trust. You become a top reviewer only if you have earned such a reputation for your advice to other customers.

Government could provide an innovation and best practice network with a similar infrastructure. The quality of an innovation and validity of a claim to good or best practice could be rated by those who had tried to transfer it, as well as by 'experts' such as researchers or OfSTED. Indeed, the trustworthiness of the judges would also be rated by practitioners, for this would be particularly important in relation to judgements or claims about high leverage and ease of transferability. For OfSTED and academic researchers to have to earn their reputation for trustworthiness would be a gain for both them and for teachers. The system would also need to give information on the location of the nearest helper-practitioner, since accessibility and opportunities for a face-to-face meeting as well as coaching and mentoring are vital. Computer-supported cooperative work (CSCW) is in its early stages but is centrally concerned with how to locate expertise and gain access to knowledgeable people. As teachers begin to use ICT for their professional development, and become more comfortable in the use of sociotechnical systems, educational CSCW will grow rapidly.

Will ICT really be a key to transformation? If it can provide what practitioners really want and need, it will. Hitherto, government has put on the pressure, but has not managed to match this with a balancing degree and quality of support. By engaging peer-to-peer self-organizing systems, the support mechanisms can be changed dramatically. The examples on the internet are already there. The incredible rise of Napster is a case in point. Napster was an internet system that allowed owners of popular music to share their MP3 collections with others. Its creator, Shawn Fanning, noticed students going to some trouble to exchange music files, so he invented the software to help them to share it easily and at no cost. This drove the Napster epidemic: millions used Napster before it ran into legal trouble over music copyright. In effect, Napster acted as a broker, using its database of who had which music files in order to link a request for a song from one PC to another PC that held the requisite file and was at that moment online – and then left them both alone to get on with their musical matchmaking. The system worked and prospered without need for altruism among users, who gave as a condition of receiving. Napster did not replace a centralised service with a decentralised one, but combined the two. It was the users who stored all the files, not Napster; but users had to go through Napster to locate what they wanted. Nevertheless, Napster, which folded in 2002, eroded the distinction between consumer and provider. Other peer-to-peer systems, such as Gnutella (originally designed to help people share recipes), do not rely on any central authority to organise the network or broker transactions. Fast-moving innovation in the peer-to-peer world is coming on stream just when the education service needs it.

The open source (or modifiable software) movement among hackers hinges on the notion that software evolves faster, becomes better and more stable as more people work on it. In a similar way, the transformation of secondary education needs innovation networks that can achieve transferred innovation much faster and over a far wider range of schools than ever before. And there might come a point – the tipping point – where there is the same exponential effect or geometric progression by which a Napster arises or a book becomes a best-seller or the mobile phone becomes a commonplace possession or the virus turns into an epidemic, all of which are transformations.

We do not yet know how to engineer such an educational epidemic that would truly qualify as a transformation. It is known how epidemics in the medical sphere work, because they have been intensively studied. We need some educational epidemiologists, as it were, to study innovation networks and uncover their dynamics. Perhaps a dedicated research centre is in order. However, we know that epidemics, and other phenomena that have tipping points, need an underlying network structure that is rich in hubs, namely the small number of super-connected individuals (our champions) who spread a disease (innovation and best practice) to many others, for example, as in the case of the early spread of AIDS. To reach the tipping point in education means inverting the way an epidemic, such as SARS, is fought. Don't break up the networks, but establish and support them; don't inhibit the champion-hubs with their many connections within the networks, but maximise their activities through incentives and recognition; don't make the environment hostile to contagion, but create a climate to foster it. The chances of successfully driving the process towards the tipping point are good, and certainly much better odds than most of the 'initiatives' that unceasingly flow from the DfES and its agencies.

Generating and sustaining networks that know how to turn ICT to their advantage is not easy, because we know too little about the dynamics of online communities, both in general as well as in education, though recent developments, such as those supported by Becta, the Networked Learning Communities in the National College for School Leadership or the Virtual Education Action Zones, will contribute substantial knowledge in the next few years. The current state of play has been well summarised by Wellman and Gulia.

The limited evidence available suggests that the relationships people develop and maintain in cyberspace are much like most of the ones they develop in their real-life communities: intermittent, specialised and varying in strength. Even in real life, people must maintain differentiated portfolios of ties to obtain a wide variety of resources. But in virtual communities, the market metaphor of shopping around for support in specialised ties is even more exaggerated than in real life... The provision of information is a larger component of online ties than of real-life ties. Yet despite the limited social presence of online ties, companionship, emotional support, services and a sense of belonging are abundant in cyberspace ... People of the Net have a greater tendency to base their feelings of closeness on the basis of shared interests rather than on the basis of shared social characteristics such as gender and socio-economic status... the homogeneous interests of virtual community participants may be fostering relatively high levels of empathetic understanding and mutual support... The distance-free cost structure of the Net transcends spatial limits

## Box 4  The power of self-organisation

Today we know that ... [r]eal networks are not static ... Instead, growth plays a key role in shaping their topology. They are not as centralised as a star network is. Rather there is a hierarchy of hubs that keep these networks together, a heavily connected node closely followed by several less connected ones, trailed by dozens of even smaller nodes. No central node sits in the middle of the spider web, controlling and monitoring every link and node. There is no single node whose removal could break the web. A scale-free network is a web without a spider. In the absence of a spider, there is no meticulous design behind these networks either. Real networks are self-organized. They offer a vivid example of how the independent action of millions of nodes and links lead to spectacular emergent behaviour.

*Albert-László Barabási*

Though it is thought of as commonplace in the arts, 'getting more out than you put in' goes against intuition in the sciences. Nevertheless, there is a real sense in which this occurs in systems that exhibit emergence ... [H]ow can the interactions of agents produce an aggregate entity that is more flexible and adaptive than its component agents? It is not an impossible question, and answers to it are certainly subject to scientific tests. It is a difficult question and one that will require sustained effort over a long period. Whatever answers we come upon will profoundly affect our view of ourselves and our world.

*John H Holland*

We're accustomed to thinking in terms of centralised control, clear chains of command, the straightforward logic of cause and effect. But in huge interconnected systems, where every player ultimately affects every other, our standard ways of thinking fall apart. Simple pictures and verbal arguments are too feeble, too myopic ... In fact, it's at the edge of what we understand today. As such, it's an ideal starting point for learning how math can help us unravel the secrets of spontaneous order, and a case study of what it can (and cannot) do for us at this primitive, thrillingly early stage of exploration.

*Steven Strogatz*

My hope and faith that we are headed somewhere stem in part from the frequently proven observation that people seem to be naturally built to interact with others as part of a greater system ... If we end up producing a system in hyperspace that allows us to work together harmoniously, that would be a metamorphosis. Though it would, I hope, happen incrementally, it would result in a huge restructuring of society. A society that could advance with intercreativity and group intuition, rather than conflict as the basic mechanism would be a major change. If we lay the groundwork right and try novel ways of interaction on the new Web, we may find a whole new set of financial, ethical, cultural and governing structures to which we can choose to belong, rather than having to pick ones we happen to physically live in. Bit by bit, those structures that work best would become important in the world, and democratic systems might take on different shapes.

*Tim Berners-Lee*

[The people at IBM] were batch-processed people, and it showed not only in their preference of machines but in ideas about the way a computation center, and a world, should be run. Those people could never understand the obvious superiority of a decentralised system, with no one giving orders: a system where people could follow their interests, and if along the way they discovered a flaw in the system, they could embark on ambitious surgery. No need to get a requisition form. Just a need to get something done.

*Stephen Levy*

[T]he regulations with which the network lives are increasingly shifting power away from the innovators and toward those who would stifle innovation ... this battle is about whose vision of creativity ... should control the future of ideas ... The forces that the original Internet threatened to transform are well on their way to transforming the Internet.

*Lawrence Lessig*

even more than the telephone, the car, or the airplane because the asynchronous nature of the Net allows people to communicate over different time zones. This could allow relatively latent ties to stay in more active contact until the participants have an opportunity to get together in person.[17]

Specialist teachers in secondary schools often have more in common with teachers of the same specialism in another school than with immediate colleagues of a different specialism. Moreover, some specialists have no, or perhaps just one, colleague of the same specialism in their school, entailing a dangerous isolation from developing best practices. Reaching other colleagues can thus be very expensive in terms of time and energy as well as convenience. The capacity of every subject specialism to create vigorous and innovative online communities and networks has yet to be fully realised. This demands that *we change the emphasis on ICT from simple communication to the development of creative communities.*

In short, at the heart of transformation are networks and online communities of educators who are passionate about transferred innovation. Like the internet, this needs no central authority; the role of government would not be to take control of it all, or administer it or even pay for it, but to help it to flourish as a system that knows how to transfer innovation and best practice laterally and then simply gets on with job. Frances Cairncross once said 'nobody owns the internet, runs it, maintains it, or acts as a gatekeeper or regulator'[18] – and it works. We should be able to say the same of the innovation and best practice network in education (see Box 4). The net is both a vehicle for transformation and a model of how it might be done, especially in the now rapid development of what Tim O'Reilly has called 'peer-to-peer solutions to big problems'.[19] Politicians' use of the very term transformation acknowledges that the problems are big: *peer-to-peer* needs to be recognised as crucial to their solution.

# 9. The fifth transformation – making a learning system

It is not merely schools that must be transformed, but some of the other institutions that serve schools and indeed exist only because of them. Their relationships also have to be transformed so that these different communities learn with and from one another.

One such is the academic community in higher education that is responsible for teacher training and most educational research. The direction of reform advocated here would require a transformation of academic educationalists and researchers, in theory and practice.

On practice, while the hacker culture marries well with that of teachers, and especially teacher researchers and teacher innovators, it is less compatible with the academic culture of higher education. Teachers and hackers both think of themselves as tinkerers who pride themselves on their craftsmanship. They tend to be modest and when publicly lauded for their achievements, as in the teachers' annual 'Oscar' awards, they self-deprecatingly attribute their success to their team or to their good fortune: they do not want to stand out from the crowd or be 'top dog'. Academics, by contrast, are in Edmund White's memorable phrase, 'alone in a private hell populated only by sycophantic graduate students, loyal colleagues and spiteful rivals'. If academic researchers want to succeed in lateral strategies, they will have to adapt their culture to blend with those of teachers and hackers.

In theory, there is little in recent academic writing that illuminates the possibility of a self-organising education system and explores what kinds of policy might be needed to initiate it and then sustain it. The *field of emergence* looks promising here. Emergence is about much coming from little, not least how complex living systems emerge from the laws of physics and chemistry. The most commonly cited example of emergence is the ant colony. Ants are simple creatures that operate according to simple rules, but they generate an overall emergent effect that vastly overshadows their individual capacities. Most important of all, the interactions of the individual components in the ant colony occur without any central control. Emergence applies to far simpler systems, such as slime mould, an extremely simple amoeba-like organism, which has been trained to find the shortest route to food in a maze despite having no central command mechanism or executive, such as a brain. Emergence also applies to far more complex systems, such as the development of self-regulating urban neighbourhoods – in which, as in a slime mould or an ant colony, the individuals are constantly replaced yet the system develops, and is able to perpetuate, a self-organizing and self-sustaining intelligence. Moreover emergence is becoming a characteristic of the internet as networks develop around it.

It is clear that the more flexible the interactions between the components of a system, and the more the components are capable of learning, the potential for emergence increases sharply: under the right conditions, they can get smarter over time. The more sophisticated the feedback systems, the greater the emergence effect. So there is the interesting question of whether, through policy, the right conditions for emergence can be created, so that emergence can be built into a complex system such as the education service, because the agents know how to exploit the underlying principles, including those of learning and feedback and, most important of all, *the capacity to learn how to learn better.*

Although emergence studies originated in biology, they now span a wide range of phenomena and are often transdisciplinary in character. This is fertile ground for academic educationalists, who might be able to explore the related subdisciplines in the field (see Figure 3). By

**Figure 3 The academic foundations of transformation**

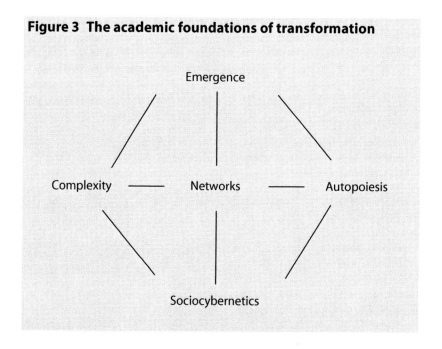

discovering leads in these new territories, we may learn how bottom-up intelligence might produce the educational transformation that will always evade an exclusive reliance on top-down managerialism.

A second group of institutions in line for transformation is at the 'middle tier' – the LEAs and the LLSCs. Estelle Morris bravely set about reforming 14–19 education and training at the very point, unfortunately, where the funding of most secondary schools would be split right in the middle of this phase, at age 16, between these two groups of bodies. Of course the system has to be made to work, but the longer-term necessity of reform of the middle tier is undeniable. The LEAs in particular have felt insecure in their role and unsure about their future. While some are not rated highly by either secondary heads or the DfES, others have over the last quarter century dramatically transformed themselves into a responsive and supportive service to their schools. Although there are continuing calls for the abolition of the LEAs, it is difficult to see how some 25,000 autonomous schools could be run from the DfES without a middle tier. In my view, the middle tier should not be reviled and then dismantled, but given a new structure and function. The LEA's role in transformation is as a hub in the network of schools in which they become a broker for networks and the disciplined innovation and knowledge transfer that needs to be coordinated within them. The middle tier of the future could play a pivotal role in creating and sustaining the social and intellectual capital of the education service. But this will not happen on the right scale without action from the centre that inspires and motivates the middle tier.

A third community that needs to be transformed is the DfES. Governments cannot leave education to look after itself, but they do have to decide how best to make their interventions in this complex public service. There are two 'ideal type' interventions that governments can make. A *directive intervention* uses legislation and regulation as the levers of change, and through them prescribes what practitioners will do. To ensure compliance, elaborate systems of inspection and accountability are introduced, and funding is carefully earmarked so that practitioners allocate resources as government intends, not as they judge appropriate locally. By contrast, an *enabling intervention* minimises legislation and external regulation, providing the infrastructure and support system on which it brokers partnerships that are self-managing but disciplined. To ensure improvement, it encourages innovation and its transfer and provides reasonable resources, which are allocated at local discretion.

It is a directive intervention that has characterised Conservative and Labour governments since 1988, and many practitioners long for change to an enabling one. It is not, of course, a question of alternatives, but of striking the right balance between the two. Transformation cannot be achieved through the directive intervention alone: it needs a new blend of the two kinds of intervention to empower the front line and transferred innovation at the heart of transformation. Ministers recognise the limits of the 'one size fits all' approach and the strategies advocated here are consistent with their policy of diversity. Just as practitioners argue for the enabling intervention to replace the directive, they plead for collaboration to supersede competition. This is another false antithesis, for the business world flourishes by a complex mixture of collaboration, in the form of strategic alliances, inter-firm networks and joint ventures, with competition to win and retain customers. This can be achieved in education too, allowing a general levelling up of quality and providing choice that is immune from allegations that diversity necessarily creates a two-tier system. Diversity is one of the preconditions for an emergent system out of which transformative innovations will spring.

The *goals* of the literacy, numeracy and Key Stage 3 strategies are similar to those of the strategy of front-line and laterally transferred innovation, but the *means* and the infrastructures are very different. With the former, the centre *announced* what had to be done (targets) and then *instructed* the teachers how to do it (the content of the strategies). With the latter, the centre has to work with the localities to *agree* what has to be done (negotiated targets) and then *discover* how best to do it through identified and transferred innovation. In the former, the model of innovation is not unlike a machine that is designed, operated, managed and controlled from the centre. In the latter the model is closer to an ecosystem that has to be cultivated, nurtured and protected in the knowledge that not everything can be controlled but there will also emerge some magical surprises.

The current model of public policy-making, argues Jake Chapman, has been based on the reduction of complex problems into separate, rationally manageable components, and is no longer appropriate to the challenges faced by governments. He advocates a systems approach to 'messy' policy areas, such as education, replete with problems that are unbounded in scope, time and resources and where there is little agreement among stakeholders about what the solutions might be and how they might be achieved. Since these very different perspectives have to be integrated and accommodated to produce effective action, the whole system has to become a learning system.[20]

While there is no question that the centralisation of educational policy-making over recent years has in England led to real improvements, this command-and-control approach has also led to some failures. Some innovations that tend towards the radical, such as the Education Action Zones, were designed from above without preparing the soil in which they were supposed to grow and with too few links to complementary reforms being promoted at that time. Education Action Zones thus had limited success, relative to costs; this weakness is difficult to acknowledge, so lessons are not being learned in the manner of an after action review.

Tom Bentley has argued that governments must learn to abandon command-and-control as the primary means of intervention to achieve progressive social ends for two reasons. First, command-and-control is simply unsuited to the complex, unpredictable demands of organisational life in the knowledge age. Secondly, command-and-control systems tend to treat people in instrumental ways in which government priorities and values are used to control others, when in fact their active consent is needed.[21] As I have argued elsewhere, school leaders have to use their organisational capital to build up the school's social capital through which its intellectual capital can be mobilised. Ministers have a parallel task to build a deeper and richer trust with teachers and other stakeholders *to enrich the system's social capital*, without which the blame culture cannot be transformed into a learning culture that fully uses its deep reservoirs of intellectual capital. As Onora O'Neill observed in her Reith lectures, fashionable methods of accountability have damaged rather than repaired trust.[22]

Restoring trust and encouraging networks as the foundations for an innovative system of secondary education does not mean that the government should leave education entirely in teachers' hands. Rather, it is a matter of creating a mix of vertical–central and lateral–local reform strategies that complement each other because they are effective in distinctive circumstances. If it wants to create busy bazaars as well as to build cathedrals, the DfES has to play a different role in this second, lateral strategy, by:

○ identifying the main areas for transformation and securing collective ownership of them

○ creating a climate of trust among the stakeholders

○ laying down an appropriate infrastructure, both social (networks) and physical (ICT)

○ encouraging schools to use this social capital to mobilise their intellectual capital in innovation

○ enhancing the organisational capital of all school leaders

○ respecting the self-organising systems and spontaneous order within the education service

○ brokering key partnerships to ensure that the process of continuous innovation and knowledge transfer thrives as the hubs change in the light of new themes and priorities for innovation.

At the heart of such a transformation is the readiness of ministers and officials in the DfES to take this role of stimulating, monitoring and helping to improve the five components of the lateral strategy described above, by a process of learning through feedback loops, so that the overall capacity of the system for continuous improvement is nourished. The relationships between ministers, their officials and practitioners will thus become transformed in line with the changed relationships within and between schools. It is difficult to exaggerate the significance of such a change; it entails some painful learning for ministers and their officials as they acquire the essential organisational capital to enrich the social and intellectual capital of the whole education service. It requires a new trust from the centre; equally, it requires a new self-discipline from those at the front line.

In short, the very system over which ministers of education preside has itself to become a more self-conscious and effective learning system in parallel to the learning organisations they advocate at grassroots level. Transformation requires everyone to learn: constantly, openly and quickly. Thirty years ago Donald Schön penned these words:

We must...become adept at learning. We must become able not only to transform our institutions, in response to changing situations and requirement; we must invent and develop institutions which are 'learning systems', that is to say, systems capable of bringing about their own continuing transformation.[23]

This is a profound lesson that has been learned in the most successful areas of business and industry, which have produced a culture of relentless innovation and the capacity to transfer it as the key to its success. The education sector must now do the same. Most important of all, the strategy outlined here paves the way to the transformation by which improvement in the education service becomes potentially self-sustaining, rather than dependent on ministerial directives and a constant stream of 'initiatives', and in the end is more efficient. Once the system, rich in intellectual and social capital, has thereby acquired a stronger and more resilient *capacity for improvement* through innovation and peer-to-peer transfer of best practice, then transformation is within our collective grasp.

# Notes

1   DfES, *New Specialist System.*
2   DfES, *London Challenge.*
3   DfEE, *Excellence in Schools,* p 12.
4   DfES, *London Challenge,* p 2.
5   Programme for International Student Assessment, Organisation for Economic Co-operation and Development, 2000.
6   DTI and DfEE, *Opportunity for All in a World of Change,* para 2.11ff.
7   DfES, *London Challenge,* p 12.
8   Huberman, 'Teacher development and instructional mastery'.
9   Collins, *Good to Great.*
10  Black et al, *Working inside the Black Box.*
11  Von Hippel, 'Sticky information and the locus of problem solving'.
12  Szulanski, *Sticky Knowledge.*
13  Berners-Lee, *Weaving the Web.*
14  Raymond, *Cathedral and the Bazaar.*
15  Kollock, 'Economies of online cooperation'.
16  Raymond, *Cathedral and the Bazaar,* p xii.
17  Wellman and Gulia, 'Virtual communities as communities', p 186.
18  Cairncross, *Death of Distance,* p 95.
19  O'Reilly. 'Remaking the peer-to-peer meme'.
20  Chapman, *System failure.*
21  Bentley, 'Letting go: complexity, individualism and the left'.
22  O'Neill, *A Question of Trust.*
23  Schön, *Beyond the Stable State,* p 30.

# Bibliography

Ackerman, M, Pipek, V and Volker, W, *Sharing Expertise*. MIT Press, 2003.

Barabási, A-L, *Linked*, Perseus Publishing, 2002.

Bentley, T, 'Letting go: complexity, individualism and the left', *Renewal*, 10(1), 2002.

Berners-Lee, T, *Weaving the Web*. Orion Business, 1999.

Black, P, Harrison, C, Lee, C, Marshall, B and Wiliam, D, *Working Inside the Black Box*. King's College London, 2002.

Brown, JS and Duguid, P, *The Social Life of Information*. Harvard Business School Press, 2000.

Buchanan, M, *Nexus*. Norton, 2002.

Cairncross, F, *The Death of Distance*. Orion Business Books, 1997.

Castells, M, *The Rise of the Network Society*. Blackwell, 1996.

Castells, M, *The Internet Galaxy*. Oxford University Press, 2001.

Chapman, J, *System Failure*. Demos, 2002.

Collins, J, *Good to Great*. Random House, 2001.

Coovert, MD and Thompson, LF, *Computer Supported Cooperative Work*. Sage, 2001.

Department for Education and Employment, *Excellence in Schools*, DfEE, 1997.

Department for Education and Skills, *The London Challenge: Transforming London secondary schools*. DfES, 2003.

Department for Education and Skills, *A New Specialist System: Transforming secondary education*. DfES, 2003.

Department for Trade and Industry and Department for Education and Employment, *Opportunity for All in a World of Change*. DTI and DfEE, 2001.

Geyer, F and van der Zouwen, J (eds), *Sociocybernetics*. Greenwood Press, 2001.

Gladwell, M, *The Tipping Point*. Little, Brown and Co., 2000.

Godwin, S, *Unleashing the Idea Virus*. Simon and Schuster, 2000.

Hargreaves, DH, *Creative Professionalism*. Demos, 1998.

Hargreaves, DH, 'A capital theory of school effectiveness and improvement', *British Educational Research Journal*, 27(4), 487–503, 2001.

Hargreaves, DH, 'Leadership for Transformation within the London Challenge', annual lecture of the London Leadership Centre, 19 May 2003.

Himanen, P, Torvalds, L and Castells, M, *The Hacker Ethic*. Secker and Warburg, 2001.

Holland, JH, *Emergence.* Oxford University Press, 1998.

Huberman, M, 'Teacher development and instructional mastery' in A Hargreaves and M Fullan (eds), *Understanding Teacher Development.* Cassell, 1992.

Illich, I, *Deschooling Society.* Calder and Boyars, 1971.

Johnson, S, *Emergence.* Allen Lane, 2001.

Kollock, P, 'The economies of online cooperation: gifts and public goods in cyberspace' in MA Smith and P Kollock (eds), *Communities in Cyberspace.* Routledge, 1999.

Levy, S, *Hackers.* Doubleday (now also Penguin), 1984.

Lewin, R, *Complexity.* Dent, 1993.

Mingers, J, *Self-producing Systems: Implications and applications of autopoiesis.* Plenum Press, 1995.

Moody, G, *Rebel Code,* Perseus Publishing, 2001.

OECD, *Knowledge Management in the Learning Society.* 2000.

O'Neill, O, *A Question of Trust.* Cambridge University Press, 2002.

O'Reilly, T, 'Remaking the peer-to-peer meme' in A Oram (ed), *Peer-to-Peer: harnessing the benefits of a disruptive technology.* O'Reilly, 2001.

Ostrom, E, *Governing the Commons.* Cambridge University Press, 1990.

Raymond, ES, *The Cathedral and the Bazaar.* O'Reilly, 1999.

Rheingold, H, *Smart Mobs.* Perseus Publishing, 2003.

Schön, D, *Beyond the Stable State.* Temple Smith, 1971.

Scrivenerr, SAR (ed), *Computer-Supported Cooperative Work.* Avebury, 1994.

Skyrme, DJ, *Knowledge Networking.* Butterworth Heinemann, 1999.

Strogatz, S, *Sync.* Hyperion, 2003.

Szulanski, G, *Sticky Knowledge.* Sage, 2003.

Taylor, MC, *The Moment of Complexity.* University of Chicago Press, 2001.

Thompson, LL, Levine, JM and Messick, DM, *Shared Cognition in Organizations.* Lawrence Erlbaum Associates, 1999.

Von Hippel, E, 'Sticky information and the locus of problem solving: implications for innovation', *Management Science,* 40(4), 429–39, 1994.

Wellman, B and Gulia, M, 'Virtual communities as communities: net surfers don't ride alone' in MA Smith and P Kollock (eds), *Communities in Cyberspace.* Routledge, 1999.

Williams, S, *Free as in Freedom: Richard Stallman's crusade for free software.* O'Reilly, 2002.

Wilson, J and Stedman Jones, D, *The Politics of Bandwidth.* Demos, 2002.